No Rhyme or Reason

V Vasanthi

First Published in April 2022

ISBN: 978-93-5628-110-3

Price: INR 200

BLUEROSE PUBLISHERS

www.bluerosepublishers.com

info@bluerosepublishers.com

+91 8882 898 898

Cover Design:

Geetika

Typographic Design:

Namrata Saini

Distributed by: BlueRose, Amazon, Flipkart

Dedicated to Smt.Savithri and Shri.Venkatraman, my loving parents ... Some people inculcate values just by practice - and teach, without actually teaching

Acknowledgements

This book is dedicated to my loving parents … so it's obvious that they are the ones whom I need to thank first … for appreciating every scribble of mine.

My sister Vijayalakshmi, a second mother, who understands me more than I do myself.

My brother Viswanathan aka Balu, whose fluency in English, I have been a secret admirer of and till date haven't been able to match and, in the process, I have become a writer.

My nephews, Sidharth, Srinath and my niece Vaishnavi who have quite often read my work and encouraged me to put it in print.

My beloved son Vidhyashankar aka, Surya, the sunshine in my life… a cheer leader and a power house of positivity whose constant support and a few sacrifices have helped me continue writing.

My husband, Ramachandran, for giving me the space to pursue my creative cravings.

My best friends, Priya and Mahalakshmi, who are my pillars of support and extended family.

Dane, my wellness mentor, for making me believe in myself and reviving my writing with his constant reassurance that my thoughts are quite relatable to many and therefore should come out.

For the team at Blue Rose who have worked on the book and brought it out in a manner exceeding my expectations.

I thank, in advance, the readers of my debut attempt.

Contents

Random thoughts

Written when I was about sixteen years. Pained by the sarcastic remarks of a taunting passer-by. After all, he wouldn't know my story!!

From Six to Sixteen

When I was six,
My mother was in a fix.
The reason being my underweight,
Which was causing everyone, a fright.

Light, I was, as a feather
My relatives did bother.
With a doctor, was fixed, an
appointment
I had to undergo, treatment.

Soon, I began to feel sick,
Because of the tonic
It made me feast,
Eight times a day, at least

The days of hardship soon followed,
As oil and ghee was all that I
swallowed
Flesh accumulated to my skin
And Lo! I was no more, thin.

Everyone was astonished,
Cos' my bony appearance vanished
Indeed, it was a long process
But still it was my doctor's success

Now I'm sixteen years,
My mother often shedding tears,
The reason being my overweight,
Which was causing everyone, a
fright

Hurried Blossoms

From buds to blossoms
Is a natural process
A fervent gardener,
waits for success.

Think of Human buds of today,
who end up learning,
the art of blossoming,
even before budding.

Woes, for them, begin,
while still in the womb
of wearied mothers
whacked by stress.

Left to the care
of proxy mothers.
Fostered or fettered?
Misted... missed, infancy.

Off to a nursery,
to acquire knowledge.
Yet as a tweeting toddler.
still not out of babbling.

Bent by the burden
of backpacks with books.
Will be hard to find, hunchbacks
only at Notre Dam

Their fingers so tender,
architects of sand castles.
are strapped to writing woods
to stay forever.

A dress code to abide by,
a schedule to chase.
Tied to the hands of the clock,
Racing against time,

No time to breathe,
no time to eat.
No time to play,
no time to be a "child".

Their nimble feet,
"Leg –cuffed" by shoe cages,
that stifle growth,
rendered shackled… stunted.

Tugged from all sides
By forces too many,
The pressure of peers
and media, to cope with.

Impelled to drift
like into a quicksand.
Like a boat without rudder
Like a horse without reins.

Learning to survive,
amidst invisible foes.
Lost in the woods
Bewildered and bereaved.

Acquiring intelligence,
at the cost of innocence.
Achieving academic success
Losing "living" in the process.

Like flowers without fragrance
and rainbow sans colours.
Like music missing melody
and marriage minus merriment.

Exiled, eliminated
Often jaded and jolted
Children like weeds,
Grown too soon.

Can we do better?
Make amends, ameliorate?
to let our buds bloom
beautifully, yet measured.

Like the chisel that turns
stones to souls
Let us shape our buds,
to flowers, that, wither not
while still to bloom
to last forever, to spray
fragrance that lingers
long after the flower is lost.

I'm Half Way Through

I'm half way through,
A journey called life.
Am I beginning to rue,
Despite there being no strife?

My mirror demands the younger me,
As streaks of grey begin to bloom,
Should I let it be?
Or is it time to groom …

From spectacular to bespectacled
From fabulous to fathomless
From unbridled to shackled
From carefree to careless

From independent to dependent
From being the giver to a taker
From confident to diffident
These thoughts send a shiver

Never before bodily change,
Never before mood swings
It is all so strange
What middle age brings!!!

The once stoic me, is lost, it seems
As emotions uncontrolled, sway
Shedding easy tears, in streams
Was never my way.

Often, clueless, I stand
As mind and brain, part ways,
Is it time to understand?
That I'm no longer in the race?

With tough choices to make,
Constant conflict inside
Maybe it's time to take a break
And quietly step aside?

Am I a good partner,
Have I found my love?
Are questions never asked thus far,
I seek answers now.

The sudden urge to connect
with friends long forgotten.
Old relationships to resurrect
and mend few broken.

Now it is me before others.
But Am I being self- centric?
Is this shift of focus,
Uncharacteristic? Or plain pragmatic?

Home is less demanding
Am I needed at all?
Work is less rewarding
Time for an overhaul

A feel of desolation
A search of purpose
Of a new me, a revelation
I realise, I'm not flawless.

As I ponder, I believe
That this is universal
There's nothing to grieve
And it is quite natural

So, it's time to relish
and age graciously
No reason to languish.
Go through this, merrily.

Remember, there is plenty
For life after forty
After all, mid-life crisis
Is no nemesis!!!

After my first visit to Rameswaram – A Jyotirlinga

Temple Beckons

As the black curtain rises,
at the first wink of the morning star
The clang of holy bells,
fragrant flowers, gorgeous garlands,
sacred saffron and towers of turmeric
Temple, beckons....

The chime of elephant bells
and cheers of children
Chants of holy mantras
and chains of devotes,
Temple, beckons....

Offerings of flowers
and clamour of coconuts, consecrated
rhythmic rendition of harmonious hymns
and serene silent prayers
Temple, beckons....

After seemingly eternal wait,
at the sight of adorned almighty
As gay tears cascade
and emotions exude
Temple, beckons....

At the radiance of lit camphor
oblivious of the surrounding,
as I move closer,
No discord of bells, I hear
No chants of prayer.
Just He and I
Temple, beckons....

With closed eyes, as I prostrate
filled with ethereal peace
The feeling forever etched in my heart,
Temple, beckons......

Learnings

Be A Butterfly

I have spent, days
Watching bubbly butterflies.
As I reflect, I realise
Imbibing butterflies, pays

Be a butterfly, in human state
spreading joy amongst many a mate.
Light in mind and body,
igniting even the moody.

Vivacious and vibrant
Eluding yet elegant.
Be a picture of poise
and an icon of grace.

You ought to be flexible,
Cos change, is inevitable.
It is a survival instinct
Lest you should become extinct.

Learn to evolve,
as times revolve.
Binge on knowledge and develop,
Take wings and gallop.

Unruffled by any storm,
Maintain your inner calm.
Have feelers to gauge,
potent perils at every stage.

Place yourself amidst, serene surrounds
Far from the bustling bounds
Be a butterfly, skirt all strife
to savour the **nectar of LIFE**.

Swing

Who could ever dislike?
A chance to turn childlike
As it came my way, today
I decided to keep inhibitions at bay.
I seized the unusual blessing
And got on to the Children's swing

As it had been an eternity,
since my last such opportunity
Despite being joyous
I was a little nervous.
I sat on the plank, firmly
and held the ropes, tightly

Slowly, as I began,
my heart didn't beat. It ran.
Upwards as it surged
and downwards as it plunged
I felt my head swivel
and my stomach, shrivel.

Soon my spirits, heightened
and my grip, fearlessly, loosened.
As I raced the breeze,
wished this moment could freeze
I was on top of the universe,
At the zenith… beyond all others

That was the child in me,
cherishing every moment with glee.
The show was over and curtains had to fall
as I had to give a chance to all.
I wish it lasted longer,
But memories would always linger.

As I got off, the adult in me pondered
On the lessons the swing offered.
Life goes up and down, back and forth
Brings joy and sorrow, gloom and mirth
It takes you high,
It makes you sigh

It is but vital
To treat all identical
To hold on to your nature
Even at the highest stature
And to remain firmly grounded
Even if not landed.

Watch Your Words

Some mouths are quivers
with words for darts,
delivered to targets, precisely.
Often too prickly.
some have whips for tongues
that lashes along.
Making a caustic penetration,
through every possible vein.
The scorching feel, begins at feet,
surging up, spreading the heat.
I hear my heart pounding.
I feel every nerve cracking.
It all takes a cyclic turn
and goes all over again.
After rounds too many
myself, I begin, to bury.
The silver cascade gushes,
breaching all barricades.
The words begin to resonate.
Can I ever recuperate?
I could have dared a scorpion's sting,
a scalpel's stabbing.
Or a viper's venom
Never mind the smarting,
A bullet can bring.
Words are far too obnoxious,
dwarfing even the virtuous.

Forgive and forget, say the wiser
Forgive, I may. Forget? Never.
I blame my memory, elephantine,
that defies all efforts of mine
to make peace with the past,
and revolting memories, to cast.
This lump in my craw,
wish, it would thaw
Cos' I'm no **Shiva**
to let it remain.
God! Why did I hear?
Give a sieve to my ear.
Grant me the might
To forget, things not right.
Whenever you blurt,
Chances are, you hurt.
So, watch your words,
Cos' they are sharper than swords.

Life Is Beautiful

How often you think
that you are driven to the brink…
To a point of no return
at the edge of a precipice.

Think again and count,
Your blessings and bouquets,
For every day in your life is a gift
and so, called – present.

Reflect on the many cheers
That wiped away your tears.
All your frets and fears,
were lost amidst fun with friends

Your windows to the world,
Helped you see nature
As God's splash of hues
On the canvas called globe.

A pair of ears to hear,
Mellifluous melodies in every sphere
All your senses brought you pleasure
and amorous memories to treasure.

Your blood, like Atlas,
carried your cares.
They laughed when you did
and comforted when you cried.

Your qualms were vanquished
and worries, buried
Amidst sweet smiles
of your blossoming buds.

The sun was here to give you warmth
The moon and stars
Like a bejewelled gown,
lit up your night.

Like pearls that drop from heaven,
raindrops moistened the earth.
Blooming gardens with
flamboyant fragrant flowers.

The endless blue sky
And the deep blue sea
Were all here to say
God loves you always.

You savoured sweet success,
your pitfalls turned experiences.
No reason to be in despair,
for you have had your worth's share.

Life is not about length,
but about the depth.
So, live your life to the fullest
Leaving all else to rest

Don't you ever conclude,
That you are the most troubled.
For the even the highest summit
may have a poignant tale, to submit.

Between the rise and fall,
are only a few years.
Make them fruitful.
For... "Life" is beautiful.

The Unstoppable

Some say I was born with dawn
But I know not my origin
I have no start spot
I neither have an end in thought
I move on perpetual.
I'm neither good nor evil,
It's what you make of me.
You desire to control me?
You'll fail. I 'am unrestrained
If treated well, I can be managed
I' am neither scarce nor in excess
To all, I grant equal access
If you lose me, it is for good
I 'am seldom understood.
Without me nothing is possible,
I am truly indispensable.
If I' am gone, its irreversible
Regaining lost me, is impossible.
I give lessons for a whole life
Some happy, some with strife
As I pass, all wounds, I heal
Scars and bruises, I repeal
I neither make you rich nor poor
I 'am a leveler for sure
I am, by all means, measurable

But I remain, at all times, invisible
I stop or wait, for none
I move on and on
Wasting me is a crime
I'm unstoppable, I am **TIME**

Tributes

My Best Friend Forever

In your lives, there would hardly be a few,
who can completely care for you.
To whom you can reach out
At any time, without a doubt

Mine is a potbellied buddy
Ever so cute and cuddly
His size shows his benevolence
And total unconditional acceptance

His best asset, his large pate
Uses it to change one's fate
He is a knowledge granary
With every trick in his armoury.

How do his eyes, so small,
Sense every woe that may befall?
To my constant rattle, he's all ears
Has been with my tears and cheers

Are his arms fore or four?
That soothe many a sore.
They're dexterous and capable
Of tasks, both light and unachievable.

When my inner state is turbulent
He shows me, this is transient.
Wonder what gives him this balance
Is it his substance or sheer silence?

He stuns you with his simplicity
That creates an instant affinity
He is the ultimate simpleton
Expecting nothing in return.

Remaining single, eternally
Makes him unique, especially
The obstacles on my pathway
He eliminates like a child's play.

He does this multi-tasking
Without me actually, asking
Of my life, he's Alpha and Omega
The good God **Ganesha**.

I Never Had Enough

I never had enough,
Of that warmth of extra covering,
That you comforted me with,
On many a cold morning.

I never had enough,
Of those ten minutes more,
That you let me sleep,
On my days, lazy and sore.

I never had enough
Of your morning coffee, hot
That had a fervent flavour,
Forever and forever in my thought.

I never had enough
Of those small meals that you made,
Filled more with love, than taste.
Those memories can never fade.

I never had enough
Of those long walks,
My hand held in yours,
and the endless talks.

I never had enough,
Of those pristine, pure whites that I wore
Often collaged by your washing
I don't wear whites, anymore.

I never had enough,
Of those words of hope
That you gave me,
When everything seemed to mope

I never had enough,
Of that infectious energy
That was uniquely yours
And caught on with me.

I never had enough,
Of that love and affection
That you benevolently bestowed
When I lay low and needed attention.

I never had enough,
Of that positive power
That you engulfed me with,
At every moment of despair.

I never had enough
Of that pride and fulfillment,
That you happily held
On my smallest achievement.

I never had enough,
Of that childlike zeal
You effortlessly exuded
To give me a joyous feel.

I never had enough
Of those mindless arguments,
That we habitually had.
They remain priceless moments.

I never had enough,
Of your childhood stories,
So humourously rendered.
That wiped off all my worries.

I never had enough
Of your commitment, unstinting
Amidst all your woes,
In abundantly, providing.

I never had enough
Of the freedom, unlimited
That you trustfully rendered.
Till today, I remain unbounded.

Maybe I should have returned more, maybe I should have thanked more,
Maybe I should have spoken more, maybe I should have loved more
Maybe I should have been a better daughter
To the best ever father.

Couldn't you have stayed longer
And made me still stronger?
Can you come back and remain?
to do it all over again?
I never had enough
Of you... **Appa**

I Have the Rarest Gem

It has been a wish
A dream that I cherished
A little short of yearning
But a thought, always
Now fulfilled, or achieved
Perhaps overwhelmed
Because, I have the rarest gem

The enduring rigidity
Dubiously masked by fascinating beauty
Evoking positive vibes,
at the first sight
An owner's delight
My aquamarine... My **Santa Maria**
Yes. I have the rarest gem

Talk about the glitter
The charm and colour
A symbol of grandeur
A sure eye turner
Undoubtedly a heart winner
My diamond – the **KOHINOOR**
Yes. I have the rarest gem

A promise of good luck
An icon of prosperity
Epitomising love for nature
A challenge to sculptors
Making others go green
My emerald.... My **Venus**
Yes. I have the rarest gem

With shimmering magnificence...
Like fire, like lightning
With all the colours of a rainbow
Reflecting my moods,
And a natural healer.
My best pal .... My **Opal**
Yes. I have the rarest gem.

Powered by lustre,
At times raw, at times cultured
Mirroring my feelings
Utterly flawless, immaculate.
Velvety smooth and serene
My white **Pearl** ... My prized possession
Yes. I have the rarest gem

An expression of unbridled love
a reflection of exuberance
Coupled with the radiance of warmth
and outstanding brilliance.
Passionate and vivacious.
My red **Ruby**...My religion
Yes. I have the rarest gem

An azure wonder
with unblemished contour
A beacon of hope, a reason to live
An instinctive protector,
A symbol of truth and candour
My true-blue **Sapphire**
Yes. I have the rarest gem

Endowed with mystical powers
Enigmatic, enchanting and enlivening
Dispelling qualms, shunning sorrow
A peace maker, a moderator
An anti-depressant
My **Topaz**… My priceless treasure
Yes. I have the rarest gem

A manifestation of myriad emotions
veiled in enthralling elegance
At times mistaken,
sometimes misunderstood
An unresolved mystery
My vivid pink **Spinel**… My soul strength
Yes. I have the rarest gem

An awesome Aquamarine
A dazzling Diamond
An enchanting Emerald
An opulent Opal
A peerless Pearl
A ravishing Ruby

A spectacular Sapphire
A scintillating Spinel
And a true Topaz
All gems wrapped together
I' am the proud owner – **A MOTHER**
Yes. I have the rarest gem

Three Letter Magic

I have always been believing
that God's way of conveying
that he loves you with all his might,
is the great gift of sight.

But only until I heard this voice,
That left me in happy tears
Do I have a choice?
Of another pair of ears

Some just sing tunes
But, when this man croons
Songs get a rebirth
Infused by his breath.

He can make your mornings, mad
He can make your evenings, sad
He can make you, anytime, happy
With his tunes so zappy

A melody for every mood,
His music can be food.
His music can mend, it can blend
To heaven, it can transcend.

He has been, at times, a father,
Many a time, a brother
Mostly a friend, at times, lover,
A respectful teacher, forever a giver.

With his childlike exuberance,
He left his listeners in a trance.
His humility, incredibly divine,
secret of his five-decade reign.

He became dearer to God
and reached the heavenly abode
Now enchanting his creator
And making heaven, heavenlier.

He may have departed
Leaving many disheartened,
His voice shall remain immortal
and continue to enthral

Gone too soon
We called him the "Singing moon"
Will this world ever get to see?
Another three-letter magic, **SPB**?!!!

It's Time To Say Thank You

For the beginning of a journey, with no destination,
For being a catalyst, in a process of transformation,
For furthering my frontiers, breaking few barriers
For making the going tough, to get the tougher me, going,
For showing that, it is okay to fall,
But not, to never rise at all.
For challenging for change, impelling to propel
For teaching that, "Patience and Consistency"
Are the keys to proficiency
For making me value progress, and to look beyond success
For showing that nothing is in vain
as pain begets gain
For enhancing my endurance, improving tolerance
For awakening my latent talents
For enduring my rants
For proving that age is no bar
Either for learning or for teaching
For believing more in me, than myself
For being a devil, ruthless
Thereby my potential, you harness
For your age defying maturity
For your impeccable professionalism
For your unstinting commitment
For being my wellness wisher,
For being a silent mentor
For being a motivator
And a hard task master

I know this journey needs to continue,
But, for the progress thus far, it's time to say Thank You!!!
Dane ... I owe this, completely, to you!!!

Invincible

It was all so, sudden
Never knew it could happen
Was the worst news to hear,
Cancer, had struck, my friend, dear.

I couldn't stop shivering
And sensed the earth, quaking
Tears left me hazy
and I was going dizzy

Feelings were mixed
Anger and anguish, alternated
"Why him?", I pondered
Could HE be so cruel, I wondered

He was all, but thirty-five
Desperately needed to survive
A daughter and wife – his family
Can he leave them, so mercilessly?

Can't count the hours
I cried under covers
With my bravest façade, possible
I decided to be with him, in trouble

It was all until we spoke,
Not he, but I, broke
I asked "Are you suffering?"
He said, "Nay. I'm fighting"

At that instant, I decided
"Cancer, you are limited"
Rummage his body, you may
but his spirits were all bright and gay.

Whenever you attacked him with vigour
He shone, like a knight in armour.
He tested your resilience
with unshakable endurance.

You crippled his parts,
but he won fonder hearts
After each of your gashes,
He soared, like phoenix, above ashes.

No amount of toxins
Could dampen his instincts
You may have left many a scar
But he pushed you really far.

As he went through his chemos
He kept you on your toes
You may have rendered him, fragile
He trounced it all, with a smile."

Today, he is no more,
Leaving many a sorrowful sore
His zeal to live, was magical
He thus remains, immortal.
He would only have died,
had he never, tried
It never was his fall
Cos' he showed to all
That the spirit isn't in the winning,
It is, but, in the running,
and it isn't the end of the rope.
There is always, HOPE.

Mahakavi

On a cold December morning,
An unknown hamlet in Tirunelveli
Saw the dawn of an awakening,
A bard, reformer, a revolutionary.

As a child, Subbaiah, he was called
His elevated thoughts, while still tender
Left one and all, enthralled,
And proved, age is just a number.

The radiance of sun, can seldom
Be shrouded by a humble palm,
This genius son of Goddess Wisdom
Could hardly be kept calm.

Captivated by his knowledge
The King called him "Bharathi"
But Bharathi left his patronage,
Shunning all pleasures, easily.

Beyond comprehension, was his brilliance
To mortal minds that crassly rebuked
He was but, a persona par excellence
Often left his decriers, spooked.

Farsighted notions, sagacious
A soul so utterly selfless
Rigid, resolute and tenacious
Pursuing visions, relentless

A crusader against casteism,
An advocate against untouchability
Amassing along many a criticism,
Defying norms, questioning authority.

Women's emancipation, his dream
Being their voice and activist
Women class, he sought to redeem
Bharathi, a modern era feminist.

Liberation of his nation,
From the shackles of slavery
Was his sole, cherished vision
and all else became secondary.

His lyrics emitted seething fire
Now anger seemed a virtue.
Inviting his adversaries' ire
Unnerved by what would ensue.

His pen, his potent weapon
When set in action, with purpose
Converged into a voice, in unison
And created moments, momentous

Bharathi, a non-violent missile
To his foes, was a nightmare
Trounced them with a smile
And routed every scare

All things pure and worthy
Become dearer to the almighty
Their end, at all times, untimely
But he lives on, immortal .... **Mahakavi**

Teachers

God was at his creative crest.
That's when he made teachers,
To keep the mankind abreast
And to procreate, achievers

A gardener who nurtures,
Seeds that soar to trees
A sculptor turning out sculptures,
From stones, with nonchalant ease.

A father, when chiding, to correct
A guide, steering to path, moral
A mother caring to protect
Teachers remain souls, immortal.

Like candles that become martyrs,
To lead from darkness to light.
Like beacons that turn torches,
On a dark moonless night.

Igniting minds, that bloom,
Moulding clay to idols.
Teachers are ones that groom.
They are eternal role models.

Treating your laurels as their own
Remaining static ladders
And a sacrificing stepping stone
That elevates aspiring leaders.

Imparting knowledge with passion
Inspiring blossoming buds to develop
Creating a whole new generation
Equipping them to gallop

Toiling to erase ignorance
Coaching to infuse life skills
Giving it, its due importance
Helping handle hurdles

Teachers are God's angels
Chosen to shower wisdom
They have no equals
They widen your spectrum.

What on earth can be a compensation
To a teacher's deeds, selfless
Gratitude is the sole reciprocation.
May God abundantly bless their class.

The Spirit of Madras

At the foot of this nation,
Adorning the Bay of Bengal,
Is the city of sensation,
Madras, we used to call.

A city that welcomes
One that generously accommodates,
And becomes comfortable homes
To folks from all states.

The vintage Connemara Library
A haven for book lovers,
Not to forget the Anna Centenary
Where every student hovers.

With one of the longest coastlines
The Marina is the city's pride
This is where the city reclines
Keeping all woes aside.

From humble roadside eateries
To restaurants, high end and quick bites
Here, one doesn't count calories
Every gastronome, Madras delights.

Idli, dosai, vadai and Pongal, yummy
Are the city's perpetual staples.
Benevolently friendly to the tummy
It is with this that the city propels

With its unique dialect
Madras thamizh, creates affinity
Its origin, none can recollect
But is here to stay for an eternity

About the heat, sweltering
Anyone who has to whine
Should also see the sea breeze, soothing
That is genuinely benign.

Home to Asia's oldest institution, technical
The College of Engineering, Guindy
And the oldest college, medical
Madras is every academician's envy

Come the Thamizh month, Margazhi
Music lovers from world over
mesmerise in mellifluous melody
Madras, an icon of cultural splendour.

If you are a movie maniac
Madras is the place to be.
Movie releases are dramatic
Amidst ardent fans' frenzy

Home of the eternal Superstar
And to The Maestro, is there a par?
Birthplace of India's Oscar star
The Mozart of Madras, ARR.

Cricket fanatics? Don't lose heart
We have the Chepauk, vibrant
Not to leave animal enthusiasts apart
It is the Vedanthangal and Vandalur, flamboyant.

With many a state-of-the-art hospital
Madras is the country's medical nucleus
Madras also is the undisputed capital
Of all activities, cultural and religious

Carrying the city's load
Madras autos are the lifeline
Like sunflowers on the road,
Endearing, by design.

Madras turns out cars, swanky
Is country's automobile encyclopaedia,
It is the growth of this industry
That makes Madras, Detroit of Asia

The city's tall temples,
Are a marvel in architecture
And are clear examples
Of heritage and culture

The rhythm of the city
Lies in its reverberating beats
Delivered with unbounded energy
Birth and death, equal, it treats

A city which is both
Modern and truly traditional
A city that none can loathe
A city that's plain practical.

A city that normally remains calm
Showed its exemplary tenacity
When nature raised an alarm
And responded with concern for humanity

Known for its simplicity
A city that shows no dearth
Of celebrations and festivity
Madras, is paradise on earth

Black

Think of all the colours of nature,
Black acquires the highest stature.
Black is utmost powerful
And equally graceful.

Totally honest in essence,
Black offers no pretence
Truly representing equality
With convincing authority.

Its ability to attract, magnetic
Remains eternally enigmatic
While other colours signify presence
Black is nothing but absence

With immense ability for absorption
There remains no scope for distortion
Black is about the depth
And conveys nothing but truth.

Black spells liberation,
It implies sophistication.
It is a sign of being regal
And always being neutral.

Black is the colour of diligence
Seldom depicts indolence.
Of self-control, it is symbolic,
Shunning all evils diabolic

Black stays in the back ground
It's a sacrifice, profound.
Black is forever, mystical
Vividly symbolising all things ethical.

It is a black board that ignites,
Minds that soar like kites.
Without the night's black banner,
Can the stars ever glimmer?

All that you own are severable
Black are shadows that are inseparable.
Black are the honest pupils,
That are mirrors reflecting scruples.

Of all the horses that trod
Black ones are the Lord
Black are the clouds that shower.
Sans them could there be a flower?

Diamonds that glitter today
Were, but, black coal, some day.
Black is the colour for a funeral
And also, for any occasion, formal.

Black doesn't differentiate
It may not radiate
But remains unique
And always, mystique

Black is impartial
It is universal
World may be colourful
But of them all, **Black** …. Is beautiful

Perspectives

I' Am Who I' Am

When the Earth was getting warmer
With overwhelming clamour and clatter
I was created as a tranquiliser
So, the World doesn't get any louder

They say I 'am reserved
From what they have observed.
I' am actually quite nerved
And can hardly get swerved

I' am at peace with myself
Which is a virtue in itself
One doesn't need no divine elf
If you look to help yourself.

Some even call me proud
And believe I sport a shroud
It's in their mind, this cloud
While, I' am just far from the madding crowd.

I have few to call as friends
With them my world ends.
Should I just follow trends,
So that the circle extends?

Like lakes that stay clear
I may seem so queer.
I' am not devoid of cheer
I restrict to only my dear

I don't come across as a cool dude
I' am mistaken, to being rude
If you think I always, brood
I deny, I just don't like any intrude.

I can never be pompous
I can never appear audacious
It is by my choice and conscious
Because, my space, to me, is precious.

While working in groups may be necessary
Some achievers do, quite the contrary
Like eagles that work solitary,
And end up being legendary.

I' am unique, I have no copy
Don't you conclude that I' am unhappy.
I' am neither grumpy nor snappy
Don't sympathise. I' am plainly happy

While all about me mayn't be overt
Also, nothing about me is covert,
You call me an introvert
I' am, but, an inward- looking expert

Inspired by the film of the same name … a humble attempt to look at the Father of the Nation, Mahatma Gandhi, from the perspective of his eldest son – Harilal Gandhi

Gandhi, My Father

It is a father who protects
He cares and directs
He is the abundant provider
And a family's leader

Mine, wasn't for me, in isolation
But a father, to a whole big nation
Pushed to a life of despair,
I was torn beyond repair

The weight of expectations
Could be the worst of tribulations.
It was my father who had principles
Am I also to follow his scruples?

A life of absolute austerity
Was his trusted ideology
A life of luxury, was my desire
Was it a sin to so aspire?

I yearned for his undivided attention,
But he toiled tirelessly for the nation.
While he took the nation forward
I was going completely wayward.

Rebellious, I naturally, turned
The scorn of the multitude, I earned
My vices followed me like a shadow
My bond with him, far from mellow

Driving him to a point of embarrassment
Was how, on him, I inflicted punishment
I gave him enough reasons to fret
And turned out to be his biggest regret

Whatever I began to reflect,
My anger it was, not disrespect
He was a father so generous,
Forgave me times, numerous.

My ways, beyond resurrection,
Cure? Only a reincarnation.
I became his son, prodigal
Was called Gandhiji's Lost Jewel

A Mahatma, he was, indeed
A father, only to me, was my need.
Can we start all over again?
Please comeback, and only mine, remain.

The Unsung Hero

It is a verity, widespread
That the lives of souls, legendary
End up famed and celebrated
And remain eternally, exemplary

Behind every life of fame
Lies an enabler in obscurity.
Do we even know their name?
Living a life of anonymity.

Talk about India's poets, supreme
His name can't be skipped
Bharathi is held in highest esteem
And is short of being worshipped.

He had a guardian Angel
His Chellamma, his soulmate.
To the world, Bharathi was a marvel
But to her? it could be a debate.

A victim of child marriage
Chellamma, wedded at seven
Impelled to face forces, savage
Marital life was far from heaven.

Bharathi was not a soul, ordinary
Almost tending to be eccentric.
Always in his world, imaginary
Oblivious to duties, domestic

No morsel of grain for tomorrow
Hunger, the family's best friend,
But Bharathi chose to feed a sparrow
Chellamma, Bharathi's godsend.

A fighter in her own right
Combating foes, invisible
None speak of her plight
Chellamma, champion incredible!!

Bharathi was different, not aligned
And she turned the haters object
Chellamma, battered and maligned
But she remained a wife, perfect.

The beauty of a tree is but evident
There's more than what meets the eye
Its strength is its roots, permanent,
That toil for tree to flourish and fortify

While you see the light, luminous
The candle, thawing, is ignored
It is a sacrifice, generous,
That renders, darkness removed.

His thoughts - pearls in an oyster
For long remained, suppressed
With none to take it further
Until, Chellamma had them inked.

Bharathi's love for Chellamma, profound
Exuded in his verses, romantic
But on print Kannamma, was found
Chellamma erased? Flawed logic.

The world rejoices Bharathi
He remained an unresolved enigma
His name, forever, etched in history
But who is Bharathi, without Chellamma?

I Am Not What You Think

If you think, I'm a lamp, petite
That's easy to be done, gusted
You'll see that I am the sun, bright
Whose shine can never be arrested.

If you think, I'm just a cloud, passing
That sprinkles a few drops random,
I am a thunderstorm, deafening
Whose power you can't fathom.

If you think, I'm but a stone, small
On a pathway that you stamp,
I am a mountain, colossal
That asks an arduous tramp.

If you think, I'm a puddle, teeny
That you can simply cross, leaping,
Sorry, it could be quite a journey
For I am an ocean, never ending.

If you think, I'm a fruit made to perish
And throw me into murky rubbish,
You're wrong. I use it to nourish,
Cos' I am a seed, born to flourish.

If you think, I'm extinguished
And out of sight, vanished
I'll come back refurbished
Because ... I am not finished!!!

Trapped

I am in a state of pursuit, to locate
The one who made rules to define
Qualities, masculine and feminine
Most of which, I freely violate.

As a girl I was always told
Don't you ever laugh aloud
For girls, that's not allowed
You need to mould.

Learn to talk in a voice, low
Never good to be vociferous
A woman needs to be gracious
There are some canons to follow

Rolling up your sleeves
And being unkempt
Were met with contempt
And were obvious peeves.

I never understood grooming
Never aligned to beauty yardsticks
Was miles away from womanly antics
Found them all, smothering.

Don't you initiate a talk
It is a masculine trait
A woman needs to wait
Or you'll draw a flak.

You got to appear docile,
Women can't be boisterous.
To appear confident is felonious,
Neither is it good to be hostile.

Growing up, I defied norms,
Remained a radical rebel.
Typecasts, I began to repel
Challenging conventions, sans qualms.

My thought process, many a time
With all efforts, I couldn't curtail
Perfectly allied with that of a male,
Never befitting a feminine paradigm

I almost always tend to align
With the views of the opposite
Sighting the underlying merit.
Is this contradiction, by design?

Should gender decide behaviour?
Are they distinct clearly?
If you see it factually,
Neither is superior or inferior.

Roles get swapped, at times
It's the man in a woman
And the woman in a man
That ring in life's beautiful chimes.

Gender is for the body, physical
The mind doesn't have any
It is this understanding, canny
That makes living, magical.

Often as I introspect, I wondered
Am I a male in a female, wrapped?
With manly thoughts. Trapped?
It remains a point to be pondered.

Relationships

No Strings Attached

When you came, you came alone
Then when these seeds were sown?
That you need a companion,
And only spouse gives communion.

Being single is not being lonely
And who says spouse means family.
Being single is being liberated
Relationships are overrated

Why is it uncanny,
to enjoy your own company?
Self-love is pure and sublime
And can grow with time.

You're spared of the need to let go
Of woes, in a relationship, that follow.
Solitude is strength not sorrow
Better single, than sorry tomorrow

No rules to breach,
No one to teach
No one to judge,
No need to nurse a grudge.

You have all the time to spare
To those who need care
Anytime they knock your door
For, singles, always care more.

Your words, you needn't tweak
You have the freedom to speak.
And when it spells inconvenience,
You have the right of silence

Being single is not being reckless
It is but being selfless.
Being more conscious, socially
And loving the world, effortlessly.

Relationships make you accommodate
They tend to suffocate
Single life is paradise
No need to compromise

Your individuality, don't you extinguish
Thereby your self- worth you diminish.
Remaining who you are is the key,
and the only secret to being free.

Chase your dreams and passions
They don't require companions.
Success or failure, whatever ensues
You have nothing to lose

It takes a lot of courage
To sever any bondage
Being single is not being detached
It is just .... No strings attached

Someone Somewhere

At the morning star's first wink,
I wake up in the pink,
The lonely bird's twitter, as I mime,
Someone...Somewhere... shares the rhyme.

In the cool breeze's whistle,
Spurred by the blithe drizzle
Water pearls, to gather, I begin,
Someone ... Somewhere... joins in

In joyous calm, and at times bad,
At happy hours or moments sad,
I search a soul that would share,
Someone... Somewhere... says "I care".

When heart rules the head
And mind gets over matter
And so, in actions, as I, err
Someone... Somewhere.... helps me alter

At times of stifling forlorn,
During its bubble sojourn
When things seem to mope,
Someone... Somewhere.... brings glimmering hope.

When into myself, I peek
And future seems bleak,
On nothings as I ponder,
Someone… Somewhere lends a shoulder.

In achievement and in dream
In darkness or in gleam
Alone as I stand,
Someone… Somewhere… holds out a warm hand.

Whether I turn a child, innocent
Or an adult, effervescent
Whatever my inner state be
Someone… Somewhere… moulds with me.

Like the soothing morning dew,
Like the rainbow's brightest hue,
Like the infinite sky, azure
Someone… Somewhere… is all serene and pure

A close companion or a person mystic
A beacon bright or a soul enigmatic
Neither a face, nor a frame
Wonder what's your name?
Whoever you are, whatever be you may,
"I know, I need you all the way"

The Unborn

After weeks of yearning
and months of longing
My wait is coming to a peak.
Yes. I'll be a mother next week
This joyous pain as I bore,
I knew it would be no more.
It would be a daughter, I decided
I would name her **"UDAYA"**
My rising sun
My sweet lil angel
I'll dress her in pinks
And think what she thinks.

These days, I have prayers
Just for mine and His ears,
May she be with beauty, blessed
And bounteous genius granted
Find her a friend, the closest ever
Let her always be a giver
Natural kindness, in her, you bestow,
Many a genial gesture, she may show.
A spirited childhood and zealous adolescence
With a pinch of maturity and a dose of innocence
From Him, I sincerely wish,
for my angel. Let her cherish

I counted down every day,
As I quietly in my couch lay
Filled with fret, frenzy and fear
I struggled to hide the odd tear
Tensed, as I close my eyes
Her rose visage and lotus feet
And the rare smile, sweet
To her warm palms and fingers tender
And to the two twinkling stars, I surrender
At this sight, as gay tears torrent
I thank Him for this moment

Days went past like years
By leaps grew my fears
Doctors' efforts went in vain
As I showed no signs of pain
A surgery, I was suggested,
The idea, I stubbornly resisted
Tired as I calmly lay,
With emotions under sway
"Mom" – I heard a voice,
"Mom", I heard it twice
It was my daughter's first call,
From within me, her wall

To her sweet song, as I hark
She spoke from the dark
"I'll leave not this nest,
to see your world that I detest.
I beseech a peaceful life,
devoid of any mournful strife.
A joyous life, where,
time permits to share and care.
I want back the lumbered trees
and the old virgin breeze.
A world sans oxygen mask
Is the least I can ask."

"I wish no wars, but peace
No deaths of disease
No child sheds a tear
No cries of hunger I hear
A roof atop every crown
a cover for every child born.
Cleanse the world of putrid poverty,
Let no barn go empty
Let there, for knowledge, be no price
Let womanhood, above all ashes, rise.
Neither nations nor frontiers be,
The globe, as one family, I wish to see."

"This is the world, I want,
To me, can you grant?"
I asked her "why don't you try,
To wipe a tear off every eye?"
At this she heaved a sigh
And said, "We can't do it, just you and I.
I said, "Udaya, you needn't be a pine in the valley,
But be a little shrub in the alley.
You mayn't be a star or moon, bright,
You can but, be, a candle light.
We may not bring a renaissance,
But, we sure, can make a difference."

"Come with fervour, amass,
Buds of your aspiring class.
Bring along the magic wand
Wield it to refresh our land.
So, don't you in despair, wither,
We can do it, together"
I spoke no further
and left the rest to her.
After the extended night, at dawn
Udaya dawned. She was born.
As I cuddled her, I had a feel,
"She's the chosen one to heal"

Mind

Mind, the Master

There is one question, universal
Answer to it, comes without a rehearsal
What do you want to be? when queried.
"Happy", is what comes, hurried.

What you want, know you may
But how to? What is the way?
Thoughts without actions, remain
Wishes or dreams, yet to attain.

If goal achievement, is your desire
A certain skill, you require
Belief in the Laws of Nature
Can bring you success, for sure.

Human mind, a tool, potent
Harness its power, inherent
Goals, when they get constant focus
Give positive results, obvious

Desire with complete conviction
As Nature's Law of Attraction
Plays a role, incredible
In making your goal, achievable.

Soak your mind, in thoughts positive
Conditioning it on the affirmative.
The forces of attraction, magnetic
Will bring you triumph, emphatic.

What your mind can conceive
It can indeed achieve
You are as high as you think
Elevate your thoughts to the brink.

Minds are mirrors that reflect
Good or evil, whatever you select
Imagine your dreams, visualize
They are successes, in disguise.

Your thoughts become words
And words become deeds
Be the master of your own mind
Aims and thoughts, get it aligned

Thoughts become things
Control what your mind brings
Keep all negatives at bay
And savour success all the way

The Wanderer

At the pinnacle of a sun kissed mountain
Wading through the cloud curtain
Engulfed in melting cream, endless
A spectacular vision in white, flawless.
I have my arms for wings… I soar
The tearing breeze, it's deafening roar
A free fall, hoping to find a plain
Landed against my wish, but not in vain
As I ended up in the sea, infinite
Naiant alongside a shoal, bright
A splash of all hues, vibrant
An exit, I did, of course reluctant.
I dart along the coast, inexhaustible
My countless footprints on sand, visible
Now I'm amidst dense woods,
Lush greenery with floral interludes.
My path leads to a desert land
Striding along the fiery golden sand
I lie with the night sky for a crown
Shimmering diamonds on a black gown
I wake up in a verdant meadow
Interspersed with many a furrow.
In pursuit of a butterfly, I glide
Discounting my weary limbs aside.
As I relentlessly ramble, I'm into
A shrine pristine, a divine rendezvous
I Stepped out to the blessing, celestial

Of water pearls that descended, mercurial
That was quite a journey, you wonder?
Possible.... 'Cos Mind is a phenomenal wanderer

Guilt

When alone, I sit in the dark,
Oft to my inner voice, I hark.
It reflects to me like a mirror,
Me, myself and my every error.

In shame, falls my head,
The future I most dread,
My guilt, through me, bites
Into the heart like termites.

To self-pity I succumb.
My guilt leaves me dumb.
The fiend gets the better of me
Oh! Will someone, set me free?

The world, at me, seems to mock,
Alone myself, I wish to lock
Tears in my eyes, fail,
When I desire to wail.

Can't I from mistakes, refrain
And forever, faultless remain?
If death can, my blemishes, delete
Let me never wake from my slumber sweet.

But I hear my conscience cry,
Why don't you give it another try?
Peace in me shall begin to dwell,
When I decide to bid guilt, farewell.

Void

The bustle has stopped,
Have I been doped?
There's an eerie calm
Is it the one before storm?

I' am in endless black spaces
Of ends, there seems, no traces.
This silence is deafening
I find myself, withering.

Walls seem to close in
Without any hint or din
Am I being smothered?
Or just hearing impaired?

Try I may, but I fail
To raise a cry or wail
I desire to flee and break free
This shackle, that's imaginary

Shaken to reality, I gather
It's only me and no other
All else is way much normal
Treading along, as usual

Life goes on for all,
Nothing seems to stall.
I' am alive yet non-existent.
This is far from transient.

I shout out. I' am accessible.
Or maybe I' am invisible?
While, all seem to operate
Am I an object, inanimate?

World moves on, automatic
While I remain, still and static
It's all so near, yet distant
Surrounded, yet vacant

It's never like before
I may be sought, no more
A little short of buried
I remain, wholly languid.

An uneasy quiet lie beneath
Like the one after death
The soul torn and toyed
Just get me out of this Void!!

Strength

Dare

You often heard people rave
That fortune favours only the brave
You need to step out of your confine
To bask in the bright sunshine.

Need to encounter paths, painful
To reach destinations, beautiful
Columbus dared to go seaward
And so, America was discovered.

There can be no ornament, intricate
Unless Gold suffers heat, ultimate.
It is the warmth and pressure, unbearable
That creates diamonds, treasurable.

The seeds buried deepest
Grow into trees, tallest.
Get trapped in an oyster shell
To become a peerless pearl.

It takes heat and hammer
To shape an iron armour
Stones endure the chisels
To turn exquisite idols.

Only after a great deal of struggle
shall the body show a muscle.
It is the high-flying Eagle
That we call the sky's regal.

Thousand pricks by a needle
Creates an exquisite ensemble.
After a metamorphosis, painstaking
Comes a butterfly's colourful making.

Unless you scale the peak, lofty
You can't see the verdant valley
Step out of your zone of comfort
Change, through conscious effort

Only what challenges
Brings welcome changes.
Be not a captive of your environment
Take courage to do things different

Do not choose the path, beaten
And end up being common.
In order to achieve feats, rare
You undoubtedly need to DARE!!!

Hold Your Head High

When times doubt your integrity
And aspersions are cast, easily
Trust yourself and none other,
Cos no one knows you better.
So, hold your head high
And meet people in the eye

A Straight tree is an easy target
But it also grows the tallest.
Black clouds may shroud the moon
But move to show the shine, soon
So, hold your head high
And meet people in the eye

Black dot on a large sheet, white
Is what the majority sight.
The vision, blinded to the larger part
Is to be imputed for its fault
So, hold your head high
And meet people in the eye

Water that flows, seems murky
Settles down to reveal its purity.
A flower's beauty doesn't vanish
Cos of a wee bit of muddy mush
So, hold your head high
And meet people in the eye

Enwrapped by snakes with venom
Sandalwood turns poison, seldom
Stones aren't subject to trials
Gems go through greater ordeals.
So, hold your head high
And meet people in the eye

Tough ones go through tough times
And emerge clean of odious grimes
The toughest soldiers are sought
For the hardest battles that are fought
So, hold your head high
And meet people in the eye

There is an inner voice that barks
Gives direction to anyone who harks
You have no one to prove but you
To yourself forever, stay true
Always, hold your head high
And meet people in the eye

Before It's Too Late

We're often so busy,
That it becomes very easy,
To push what you need to do today,
To an unknown someday.

Someday, is not a day of a week
It's often a sign of the weak
Time and tide wait for none, they say
So do it without further delay

You wanted to say a Sorry,
But thought, What's the hurry?
Don't look for the right date
Say it … Before it's too late.

Wished to give someone a hug?
And you gave the thought a shrug?
You cannot predict fate,
Hug them … Before it's too late.

How often have you desired?
to have a long talk, heart to heart?
There's no right time for a tete a tete.
Talk … Before it's too late.

Cooking someone's favourite dish,
Could have been a long pending wish.
It's easy to delight a palate,
Do it ... Before it's too late.

Want to mend some broken tie,
Want to wipe a tear off an eye,
Make amends, ameliorate
Fix it ... Before it's too late.

You wish to express love
But never knew how,
It's time to demonstrate
Love .... Before it's too late.

Feel like forgiving a person
Who became a foe, for no reason?
Let the poison not aggravate
Forgive ... Before it's too late.

Unfulfilled promises are millstones
That are hard on your backbones
It's felonious to procrastinate
Fulfil them ... Before it's too late.

How often you held back a Thank You,
From someone to whom it is due?
Don't you ever hesitate
Thank ... Before it's too late.

Desired to gift a beloved
And to see them overwhelmed
A mere thought is inadequate,
Gift … Before it's too late

Learn to appreciate what you have
Before it becomes, what you had.
Don't give room for any regret
Value it … Before it's too late.

Unfulfilled desires, dreams truncated
Occupy one's mind and can't be vacated
So, what makes you wait?
Finish, fulfil, accomplish … Before it's too late

Just go with the Flow

We are often so desirous
Of always wielding the reins
And feel absolutely fabulous
When control, with us, remains

To this end, we design and direct
All our thoughts and activities.
If this was always so perfect,
Shouldn't success come with guarantees?

Sometimes it isn't about control
There's a certain pleasure, puzzling
While taking a gentle stroll
In life, as it keeps coming.

Go with the tide, rise and fall
Experience the highs and lows
Neither is going to be a long haul
May end up in mountains or meadows.

Life is about experience,
Don't seek to regulate.
Have no worries about prudence
Eventually nothing can be accurate

Our entry was not planned
Neither can your exit be
Life's journey cannot be manned
This insight, sets you free

A river that flows, merrily
Doesn't think of its destination
Just enjoys the whole journey
Seeking no adulation.

Swayed by the winds, ravenous
The clouds meander, in the sky.
May end up calm or thunderous
Do they ever wonder why?

When your soul seeks succour
The tears, cascading, eases
Allow it to completely devour
All your qualms and bruises.

How often it has happened,
Your efforts ended up empty,
And when you thought it was the end,
Got a leash of free -flowing energy.

It is never an act of wisdom
To stop the flowing current
Leaving some things to the system
Could be the best judgement

So, sit back and just enjoy the feel
Anyways you can't plant a rainbow
Life has a lot more to reveal
You ... Just go with the flow!!

Faith

When you are driven to the brink
and the going gets tough
There is a force, that,
gets you, tougher than the going.
It gives you an extra edge
and keeps you from withering.
It has moved mountains
has powered revolutions.
It has defied diseases
often defeated, death
Has turned visions
to illustrious victories.
It is the flame,
that braves tempests
The hummock, that,
humbles thunderstorms.
What may have been a debacle,
It transforms to, a miracle.
To believe in something
is the muscle behind glory.
Faith is this force
that gives you the vim and vigour
to fetch the far-fetched
to do the incredible.
It is the Star of Wonder
That helps you see light,
at the end of the tunnel.

It is a precious treasure,
no Shylock can covet.
Can neither be earned or loaned,
Nor borrowed or bequeathed
Never ages with age
remains robust, eternally.
The path to success
is never a bed of roses
Faith is the catalyst, that,
sails you through,
Nurture it, feed it, nourish it,
Let it be live and kicking,
Faith is the soul strength,
Keep it glowing.

9 789356 281103

Printed by Libri Plureos GmbH in Hamburg, Germany